n or before

Insects in the Pond

This book has been reviewed
for accuracy by
Walter L. Gojmerac
Professor of Entomology
University of Wisconsin—Madison.

595.7

Library of Congress Cataloging in Publication Data

Oda, Hidetomo.
  Insects in the pond.

10533

  (Nature close-ups)
  Translation of: Ike no konchū / text by Hidetomo
Oda, photographs by Hidekazu Kubo.
  Summary: Discusses how diving beetles, water
scorpions, dragonflies, and other insects play an
important role in maintaining a pond's ecosystem.
  1. Insects, Aquatic—Juvenile literature. 2. Pond
fauna—Juvenile literature. [1. Insects, Aquatic.
2. Pond animals. 3. Pond ecology. 4. Ecology]
I. Kubo, Hidekazu, ill. II. Title. III. Series.
Q L467.2.03313 1986   595.7'0526322   85-28227
ISBN 0-8172-2529-3 (lib. bdg.)
ISBN 0-8172-2554-4 (softcover)

This edition first published in 1986 by Raintree Publishers Inc.

  3 4 5 6 7 8 9 0   90 89 88

Insects in the Pond

Raintree Publishers
Milwaukee

▶ **Hints on collecting pond insects.**

Take a net and a pail with you to a nearby pond. Ponds that have a lot of plant life, such as cattails and waterweed, will have more kinds of insects than ponds with little vegetation.

◀ **This long-legged water scorpion is so well disguised that it resembles the dead branch on which it is hiding.**

If you have ever tried to catch fish in a pond, you know that more than just small fish live there. As you scoop up the net, you may notice flatworms, diving beetles, dragonfly larvae, or other insects buried in the pond silt. The lives of all these pond creatures are closely interrelated. They all depend on one another, in some way, for survival. Each pond resident contributes, in its own way, to the life cycle of the pond.

There are ponds all over the countryside. Some are natural ponds, in meadows, mountains, and marshes. Other ponds are made in parks and on farms and ranches by people. But they all have one thing in common—they are full of all kinds of plant and animal life.

It is fascinating to watch pond animals interact with one another. But for several reasons, it is often difficult to observe pond life. Because many ponds are surrounded by cattails and other plants, they are hard to get to. Also, the surfaces of ponds are often covered with a cloudy film of scum, or algae, which makes it difficult to see into the water. And, many pond insects are impossible to see from the surface because they stay hidden beneath waterweeds and other pond plants.

But if you catch some insects, you can take them home and keep them in a fish tank, in your own pond-aquarium, and watch them closely.

● **Stocking the aquarium.**

The insects you catch may eat one another. So put some waterweed in your pail to provide hiding places for them, or carry them home in different containers. ("Let's Find Out" at the back of this book tells you how to make an insect aquarium.)

▲ Try to find the insects below in the aquarium photographed above.

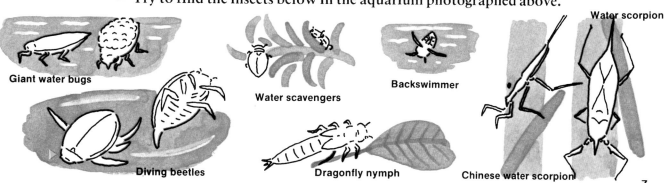

Giant water bugs

Water scavengers

Backswimmer

Water scorpion

Diving beetles

Dragonfly nymph

Chinese water scorpion

▲ **Water striders patrolling the water's surface.**

Water striders feed on insects that drop onto the pond's surface. When an insect falls into its territory, the strider quickly skates over and seizes its prey.

▶ **Close-up of a water strider.**

The water strider's long legs enable it to move quickly across the water's surface.

Water striders are dark, slender, long-legged insects that skate about on the pond's surface. They have three pairs of legs. The middle pair is used for "rowing" across the water's surface. The back legs are used for steering. The water strider's front legs are used for catching prey. The insect's body is coated with oil, particularly on its underside. The oil repels the water and enables the water strider to move across the pond's surface without breaking through. Because they have adapted so well to life on the water, some kinds, or species, of water striders have lost the use of their wings and can no longer fly.

▼ A water strider preying on a fallen moth.

The surface of the pond is like a giant net in which the water strider catches insects. When a moth falls into a pond, its wings become wet and it is trapped in the water. With its needle-like mouth, or proboscis, the strider sucks the moth's body fluids.

▼ A backswimmer attacking a water strider.

The backswimmer reaches up with its clawed front legs and seizes this water strider on the pond's surface. Backswimmers hunt, or prey upon, insects that have fallen into the pond and those which move across its surface.

▶ A backswimmer eating a water strider.

Like all true bugs, the backswimmer has a long needle-like proboscis. It pierces its victim, the water strider, and sucks its body fluids.

▲ A backswimmer lying in wait.

The backswimmer in its upside-down position, waiting for prey.

Another pond inhabitant is the backswimmer. True to its name, this water bug swims upside down on its boat-shaped back as it paddles its back legs.

The backswimmer stores air for breathing in two grooves in its abdomen, the rear part of its body. The stored air makes the bug light and enables it to float upside down just beneath the surface of the pond. The backswimmer comes to the surface from time to time to rest and get a new supply of air.

The backswimmer is an enemy of the water strider and other insects. It floats on its back, just below the water's surface, waiting for a chance to attack tadpoles, adult insects, and insect larvae.

Plant life in ponds is rich and varied. All green plants, from tiny algae to large, flowering pond lilies, play a vital part in the food chain of the pond. The green plants are food for the plant-eating animals and water insects. These animals, in turn, are preyed upon by carnivorous, or meat-eating, animals.

But pond plants serve another function, as well. The roots, ferns, dead leaves, and waterweeds at the pond's bottom provide places for water insects to hide from preying birds, fish, and from each other.

▼ **A bagworm crawls among the waterweed.**

This caddisfly larva spins a soft silk casing for itself and attaches bits of leaves and plant debris to it. Its bag-like home keeps it well hidden from predators.

▼ **A shrimp hides among the waterweed.**

Not only insects, but also small fish and other creatures live among the waterweed where they find both food and shelter.

▲ Two Chinese water scorpions.

Chinese water scorpions are not good swimmers. They move about underwater by clinging to waterweeds and dead branches. Because their stick-like bodies look like branches, they are well hidden from enemies.

▲ **A Chinese water scorpion attacking a tadpole.**

The Chinese water scorpion reacts only to things that move. It waits for victims to come its way. As the photos show, the scorpion is not always successful in its attacks.

Although the Chinese water scorpion spends most of its life on the pond's bottom, it cannot swim well. When it does travel, it uses its long middle and hind legs to make its way along waterweeds and dead branches. But most of the time it remains still, poised on a branch, waiting for prey to pass by. Because the scorpion's stick-like body looks like a branch, it is well-hidden, or camouflaged, as it waits.

The Chinese water scorpion is carnivorous. When a tadpole or small fish swims near, the scorpion lifts its front legs in readiness. Then, bending forward, it extends the hooks on its legs. If it is quick enough, the water scorpion can catch its prey.

▶ **A Chinese water scorpion catches a tadpole.**

The water scorpion uses its needle-like proboscis to pierce its victim and suck its body fluids. It does not tear its victim to pieces, as does the praying mantis, a similar insect which lives on land.

Although the Chinese water scorpion looks like a dead branch, this species of water scorpion looks more like a leaf or a piece of decaying wood. The two kinds of scorpions belong to the same insect family, the Nepidae family.

Like other pond insects, water scorpions need oxygen to breathe—without it they would die. Members of the Nepidae family breathe through a long tube that extends from the base of the abdomen. Occasionally, the insects rise to the top of the pond and stick their tubes above the pond's surface to get a new air supply.

▶ **A water scorpion catches a minnow.**

The water scorpion uses the large hooks on its front legs to seize its prey, a minnow.

◀ **The water scorpion's breathing tube.**

The thin tube that extends from the scorpion's abdomen is used for breathing. The scorpion sticks it above the water and takes in oxygen from the air.

▲ A tiny water scorpion emerges.

The female water scorpion lays her eggs in the spring. Two weeks after they are laid, the nymphs emerge.

The female water scorpion comes out of the water to lay her eggs. She deposits them on bog moss or on soft, decaying plants on the surface of the pond. Long, slender breathing tubes extend from the eggs. Each egg has two to nine tubes, depending on the species of water scorpion.

When the nymph emerges from the egg, it looks just like a tiny adult water scorpion. It is able to catch prey, just as the adult does. But it must grow much larger and shed its old skin many times before it finally becomes an adult insect with large wings.

▶ Water scorpion nymphs eating a midge larva.

The newly emerged nymphs soon begin to catch and eat insects at the edge of the pond or in shallow pools of water.

◀ A giant water bug carrying eggs.

After the female has laid the eggs on his back, the male carries them around with him as he swims through the pond. Nymphs usually emerge from the eggs within a few days.

▼ A giant water bug nymph emerges.

Another pond insect is the male giant water bug. It is among the best babysitters in the insect world. The female climbs onto the male's back to lay her eggs. She secretes a sticky substance which glues the eggs securely to him. The male carries the eggs on his back in the pond until they hatch.

The female may lay from 150 to 175 eggs at a time. She sometimes has to find two or three males to carry all her eggs. Or, she may wait until the first brood hatches. Then she carefully removes the empty eggshells from the male's back before laying more eggs.

▼ The female giant water bug laying her eggs.

After the female has laid her eggs on the male's back, he cares for them. He swims in the warm shallows of the pond to keep the eggs at the right temperature. And he goes to the surface of the pond often so they can breathe.

▲ **A diving beetle among the waterweeds.**

The diving beetle swims by paddling its back legs like the oars of a rowboat.

▲ **Diving beetles eating a crayfish.**

Its odor attracted a number of diving beetles to this dead crayfish.

Diving beetles are known as the cleaners of the pond. They are attracted by the smell of dead and decaying flesh. Diving beetles eat every part of an animal's remains—even hair, feathers, skin, and particles of bones.

The diving beetle, like the water scorpion and other pond insects, must breathe oxygen from the air. It often swims to the pond's surface where it hangs head down, with the tip of its abdomen sticking out of the water. It traps air and stores it beneath its wings before diving back into the water.

◀ Water scorpions take in air through a snorkel-like tube.

▶ Diving beetles store air beneath their wings and carry it with them. Similarly, a scuba diver breathes stored oxygen.

▼ **A diving beetle carrying a crayfish pincer.**

Diving beetles have strong pincer-like jaws, mandibles, which enable them to break up tough objects like crayfish. The arrow shows waste material leaving the beetle's body.

◀ **A water scavenger eating a decaying plant.**

Many kinds of beetles live in ponds. The water scavenger beetle adult looks a lot like the adult diving beetle.

▼ **Beetle larvae attacking live prey.**

A water scavenger larva (left) and a diving beetle larva (right). These larvae have strong jaws for seizing their prey.

Many insects go through physical changes as they develop. Some insects, like water scorpions, go through three stages: egg, nymph, and adult. Scientists call this an incomplete metamorphosis because the nymph looks very similar to the adult insect. Other insects, like diving beetles, go through four definite stages: egg, larva, pupa, and adult. Scientists call this a complete metamorphosis.

When a diving beetle larva emerges from the egg it looks quite unlike the adult beetle. The larva has a long, thin, caterpillar-like body. It crawls around on the bottom of the pond, eating live insects. Soon, the larva leaves the pond and crawls up on land. It burrows into the ground, sheds its skin, and becomes a pupa. During this resting stage, important changes are taking place. A fully developed, adult diving beetle will eventually emerge.

▼ **A diving beetle pupa.**

The larva burrows into the earth and makes a small nest for itself. It sheds its skin and becomes a pupa.

▼ **The pupa becomes an adult.**

When the adult beetle emerges, it waits until its wings have dried and hardened. Then it leaves its nest and returns to the pond.

▲ **A dragonfly nymph waits for prey.**

This nymph has buried itself in the mud at the bottom of the pond as it watches for prey.

▲ **The nymph's coloring blends with the background.**

When a large animal approaches, this nymph has only to bury its head in the mud to be well hidden.

This funny looking creature is a dragonfly nymph. It crawls on the bottom of the pond, hidden in the mud. One day it will be flitting above the water on beautiful, delicate wings. The nymph is the second stage in the dragonfly's life cycle.

The dragonfly nymph is a fierce underwater predator. It stalks its prey among the waterweeds at the bottom of the pond. The nymph has a unique lower lip called a labium. The lip forms a kind of mask between its two, large, bulging eyes. The labium unfolds and reaches out with incredible speed to capture insect larvae, worms, and small animals that swim by.

How nymphs breathe.

Damselfly nymphs, cousins of dragonflies, breathe through gills in the ends of their abdomens.

Dragonfly nymphs breathe with gills, using water drawn in at the tip of the abdomen.

▼ **A dragonfly nymph catches a small fish.**

The dragonfly nymph feeds on small pond animals. In turn, the nymphs are preyed upon by giant water bugs and other insects.

▲ **A dragonfly emerges.**

After the adult has left the old skin it hangs upside down and rests. Then it curves its body forward and pulls itself up onto the old discarded skin and waits for its wings to harden.

The larval stage is the longest in the dragonfly's life cycle. It may last from several months to five years, depending on the species. When the nymph has fully developed, it leaves the pond for the first time in its life. It climbs onto a branch or plant stem above the water's surface. Soon, a change begins to take place.

The dragonfly nymph's old skin splits down the back and the adult's body begins to emerge. First the head, with its large eyes, appears. Then the thorax, or midsection, comes into view, with its long legs and crumpled wings. Finally, the long, segmented abdomen is pulled slowly from the old skin. Within hours, the wings harden and dry and have become full size. The adult dragonfly is ready to begin the final phase of its life—in the bright sunshine above the surface of the pond.

Let's Find Out

How to Keep Pond Insects

An insect aquarium.

Put your aquarium near a window but protect it from direct sunlight. You may also use a fluorescent light. It may be necessary to use an air pump to add oxygen to the water.

A pond aquarium should have waterweed and dead branches to serve as hiding places. It must also have sunlight. And it must have the right kind of food for the insects you decide to raise.

When the adult insects have laid their eggs and the larvae have emerged, the larvae should be put in a separate tank. Otherwise, the small larvae will be eaten by the larger insects. Put a net over the top of the adult insects' aquarium to keep them from flying away at night.

Collect what you need for your aquarium from a pond or river, but rinse everything off before putting into your aquarium. If you use tap water, put it in the sun for a day or so before you put it in the aquarium.

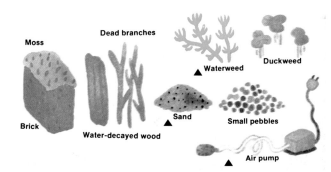

Feed Some Insects Prey.

Some insects, like dragonfly nymphs, backswimmers, and water scorpions, are predators. You can feed them tadpoles, mosquito larvae, or raw fish.

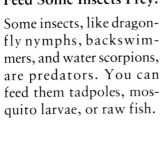

Tadpoles

Small fish

Midges

Worms

Raw fish

A diving beetle larva eating a dragonfly nymph.

A water scorpion larva eating a midge larva.

Food for Diving Beetles and Water Scavengers.

Feed adult diving beetles dead fish, small dried fish, etc. Water scavengers eat waterweed. Remove the food leftovers every day from the aquarium so the water doesn't become stale.

◀ Grey diving beetles gathering around a dead fish.

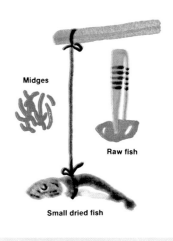

Midges

Raw fish

Small dried fish

Observing a Dragonfly Emerge.

When the dragonfly nymph has grown large and stops eating, it will soon begin to emerge. Put a dead branch in the aquarium. Be sure that the branch sticks out of the water. After dark, when the dragonfly nymph begins climbing the stick, wait patiently and watch as the adult dragonfly begins to emerge.

An aquarium for dragonfly nymphs.

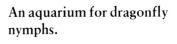

◀ An adult dragonfly emerges.

GLOSSARY

algae—pondscum, seaweed, and other primitive forms of water vegetation. (pp. 6, 12)

camouflage—to hide by blending with the environment. (p. 14)

carnivorous—a word used to describe animals that eat meat. (p. 14)

labium—the unique lower lip of an insect. (p. 26)

mandibles—jaws which are used for biting and chewing. (p. 23)

metamorphosis—a process of development during which physical changes take place. Complete metamorphosis involves four stages: egg, larva, pupa, and adult. Incomplete metamorphosis occurs in three stages: egg, nymph, and adult. (p. 25)

prey—animals that are hunted and killed by other animals for food. (pp. 8, 11, 18)

proboscis—a tube-like mouth used for sucking liquids. (pp. 9, 11, 14)

species—a group of animals which scientists have identified as having common traits. (pp. 9, 18)

thorax—an insect's midsection to which legs and sometimes wings are attached. (p. 28)